Programmatic SEO

How to Leverage Automation and Data Science for Better Search Engine Rankings

I0479792

By Hugh Webb

Disclaimer:

The information provided in this book is for educational and informational purposes only. The author is not a licensed professional, and the content should not be considered a substitute for professional advice or services. The reader assumes full responsibility for any actions taken based on the information in this book. The author and publisher are not liable for any damages or negative consequences arising from the use or misuse of the information provided. It is recommended that readers conduct their own research and consult with a professional before making any significant changes to their cleaning routine or use of natural cleaning products.

Table of Contents

Chapter 1: Definition of Programmatic SEO and Its Benefits
Search engine optimization (SEO) is an essential aspect of digital marketing that involves optimizing websites and online content to rank higher in search engine results pages (SERPs). Programmatic SEO, also known as automated SEO, is a modern approach that leverages automation and data science to enhance SEO performance.

Programmatic SEO involves using algorithms and software to automate various aspects of SEO, including keyword research, content optimization, link building, and analytics. With programmatic SEO, marketers can optimize their SEO efforts more efficiently, and at scale, resulting in improved search engine rankings, increased organic traffic, and higher conversion rates.

Benefits of Programmatic SEO
1. Increased Efficiency: Programmatic SEO automation reduces the time and effort required for SEO optimization. This means that marketers can focus on other essential aspects of their digital marketing campaigns, such as content creation and engagement.
2. Better Keyword Research and Mapping: Programmatic SEO tools provide more precise and comprehensive keyword research results than manual keyword research. Marketers can use these tools to identify keywords that are relevant to their target audience and optimize their content for these keywords, resulting in better search engine rankings and higher organic traffic.
3. Enhanced Content Optimization: Programmatic SEO tools can analyze content to identify areas that need optimization. These tools can evaluate content quality, readability, and relevance to ensure that it aligns with the target audience's needs and preferences.

4. Improved Link Building: Programmatic SEO can automate the link building process, allowing marketers to secure high-quality backlinks more efficiently. Automated link building ensures that the links are relevant, trustworthy, and natural, resulting in better search engine rankings and more organic traffic.
5. Real-time Analytics and Reporting: Programmatic SEO tools provide real-time analytics and reporting, allowing marketers to monitor and evaluate their SEO performance and make data-driven decisions. This helps them optimize their SEO efforts continuously, resulting in improved search engine rankings and better business outcomes.

Conclusion

Programmatic SEO is a modern approach that enables marketers to optimize their SEO efforts more efficiently and at scale. It offers various benefits, including increased efficiency, better keyword research and mapping, enhanced content optimization, improved link building, and real-time analytics and reporting. Marketers who embrace programmatic SEO can improve their search engine rankings, increase organic traffic, and achieve better business outcomes.

Chapter 2: Historical Overview of SEO Automation

Search engine optimization (SEO) automation has been evolving since the early days of search engines. In this chapter, we will take a look at the historical overview of SEO automation, its milestones, and how it has changed the SEO industry.

Early Days of SEO

The first search engines, such as Archie and Gopher, were launched in the early 1990s. These search engines used basic algorithms to crawl and index websites, allowing users to search for information. At this time, SEO was in its infancy, and marketers mainly focused on using basic techniques such as keyword stuffing, meta tags, and link farming to rank their websites higher in search engine results pages (SERPs).

The Rise of Google and SEO Automation

In the early 2000s, Google emerged as the dominant search engine, and the SEO industry began to evolve rapidly. Google's algorithm updates, such as Panda, Penguin, and Hummingbird, forced marketers to rethink their SEO strategies and focus on providing high-quality content and natural link building.

With the increasing complexity of SEO, marketers began to develop software and tools to automate various aspects of SEO. One of the earliest SEO automation tools was WebPosition Gold, which was launched in 1995. WebPosition Gold allowed marketers to track their website's search engine rankings, monitor their competitors' rankings, and automate various aspects of SEO, such as keyword research, link building, and analytics.

SEO Automation in the Modern Era

In the last decade, SEO automation has continued to evolve, driven by advances in data science, artificial intelligence, and machine learning. Today, there are numerous SEO automation tools and platforms available, including SEMrush, Ahrefs, Moz, and Google Analytics.

These tools enable marketers to automate various aspects of SEO, including keyword research, content optimization, link building, and analytics. Automation has made it possible for marketers to optimize their SEO efforts more efficiently and at scale, resulting in improved search engine rankings, increased organic traffic, and higher conversion rates.

Conclusion

SEO automation has come a long way since the early days of search engines. As search engines become more sophisticated, marketers have been forced to adapt and develop new strategies to improve their search engine rankings. Automation has played a vital role in this evolution, enabling marketers to optimize their SEO efforts more efficiently and at scale. Today, SEO automation is a critical component of any successful digital marketing strategy.

Chapter 3: The Evolution of Programmatic SEO

Programmatic SEO has undergone a significant evolution in the past few years, driven by advances in data science, artificial intelligence, and machine learning. In this chapter, we will explore the evolution of programmatic SEO and how it has changed the SEO industry.

Early Days of Programmatic SEO

The early days of programmatic SEO were characterized by basic automation tools that enabled marketers to automate various aspects of SEO, such as keyword research, content optimization, and analytics. These tools were limited in functionality and were mainly used to reduce the time and effort required for SEO optimization.

The Rise of AI and Machine Learning

In recent years, the rise of AI and machine learning has revolutionized programmatic SEO. AI-powered SEO tools use advanced algorithms to analyze data and provide insights into various aspects of SEO, such as keyword research, content optimization, and link building.

One of the most significant advances in programmatic SEO is the use of natural language processing (NLP) algorithms to understand and analyze user intent. NLP algorithms enable SEO tools to analyze the language used by users when searching for information and provide more relevant search results.

Another significant advance is the use of machine learning algorithms to analyze search engine algorithms and predict how they will rank websites. Machine learning algorithms enable SEO tools to analyze vast amounts of data and provide insights into how search engines work, allowing marketers to optimize their websites and content accordingly.

The Future of Programmatic SEO

The future of programmatic SEO is exciting, with new advancements being made every year. One area of significant potential is the use of voice search optimization, which is becoming increasingly popular with the rise of smart speakers and virtual assistants.

AI-powered SEO tools are also becoming more intelligent, with the ability to understand and analyze complex data sets. This will enable marketers to optimize their SEO efforts more efficiently and at scale, resulting in improved search engine rankings, increased organic traffic, and higher conversion rates.

Conclusion

Programmatic SEO has come a long way in a short time, driven by advances in data science, artificial intelligence, and machine learning. These advancements have revolutionized the SEO industry, enabling marketers to optimize their SEO efforts more efficiently and at scale. The future of programmatic SEO is exciting, with new advancements being made every year, and it is sure to play an essential role in the future of digital marketing.

Chapter 4: Assessing Current SEO Performance

Assessing your current SEO performance is crucial to optimizing your website for search engines. In this chapter, we will explore the various tools and techniques used to assess current SEO performance.

Keyword Analysis

Keyword analysis is an essential component of SEO performance assessment. It involves analyzing the keywords that are driving traffic to your website and determining how well your website is ranking for those keywords.

There are numerous tools available for keyword analysis, such as Google Analytics, Google Search Console, SEMrush, Ahrefs, and Moz. These tools enable you to analyze the keywords that are driving traffic to your website, track your website's search engine rankings, and identify areas where you can improve your SEO efforts.

Content Analysis

Content analysis involves analyzing the quality of your website's content and determining how well it is optimized for search engines. This includes analyzing the structure of your content, the relevance of your keywords, and the readability of your content.

There are several tools available for content analysis, such as Yoast SEO, SEMrush, and Ahrefs. These tools enable you to analyze your website's content and provide recommendations on how to optimize your content for search engines.

Backlink Analysis

Backlink analysis involves analyzing the number and quality of websites that link to your website. Backlinks are a critical component of SEO, as they signal to search engines that other websites find your content valuable and relevant.

There are several tools available for backlink analysis, such as Ahrefs, SEMrush, and Moz. These tools enable you to analyze your website's backlinks, identify low-quality links, and track your website's link-building progress.

Technical SEO Analysis

Technical SEO analysis involves analyzing the technical aspects of your website and identifying areas where you can improve your website's performance. This includes analyzing your website's load speed, mobile responsiveness, and website architecture.

There are several tools available for technical SEO analysis, such as Google PageSpeed Insights, Google Search Console, and SEMrush. These tools enable you to analyze the technical aspects of your website and provide recommendations on how to improve your website's performance.

Conclusion

Assessing your current SEO performance is crucial to optimizing your website for search engines. Keyword analysis, content analysis, backlink analysis, and technical SEO analysis are all essential components of SEO performance assessment. By using the right tools and techniques, you can identify areas where you can improve your SEO efforts and optimize your website for search engines.

Chapter 5: Identifying SEO Objectives and KPIs
Identifying SEO objectives and key performance indicators

(KPIs) is essential for measuring the success of your SEO efforts. In this chapter, we will explore the process of identifying SEO objectives and KPIs.

Defining SEO Objectives
The first step in identifying SEO objectives is to define the goals you want to achieve with your SEO efforts. Some common SEO objectives include:
1. Increasing website traffic
2. Improving search engine rankings
3. Boosting brand visibility and awareness
4. Generating leads or sales

Once you have defined your SEO objectives, you can begin to identify the KPIs that will enable you to measure your progress towards achieving these goals.
Identifying SEO KPIs

SEO KPIs are metrics that enable you to measure the success of your SEO efforts. Some common SEO KPIs include:
1. Organic search traffic: This measures the number of visitors who find your website through search engine results pages (SERPs).
2. Keyword rankings: This measures how well your website ranks for specific keywords.
3. Backlinks: This measures the number and quality of websites that link to your website.
4. Click-through rate (CTR): This measures the percentage of clicks your website receives compared to the number of impressions it generates.
5. Conversion rate: This measures the percentage of website visitors who take a desired action, such as filling out a form or making a purchase.

It is important to choose KPIs that align with your SEO objectives and provide meaningful insights into the success of your SEO efforts.

Setting Targets and Benchmarks
Once you have identified your SEO objectives and KPIs, the next step is to set targets and benchmarks for each KPI. Targets are the specific numbers or metrics you want to achieve for each KPI, while benchmarks are the current performance levels for each KPI.
By setting targets and benchmarks, you can measure your progress towards achieving your SEO objectives and adjust your SEO strategy accordingly.

Conclusion
Identifying SEO objectives and KPIs is essential for measuring the success of your SEO efforts. Defining SEO objectives, identifying relevant KPIs, and setting targets and benchmarks for each KPI can help you measure your progress towards achieving your SEO goals. By regularly monitoring and adjusting your SEO strategy, you can optimize your website for search engines and achieve your desired SEO outcomes.

Chapter 6: Setting up a Programmatic SEO Framework

Setting up a programmatic SEO framework is crucial to optimizing your website for search engines. In this chapter, we will explore the process of setting up a programmatic SEO framework.

1. Define Your SEO Strategy

The first step in setting up a programmatic SEO framework is to define your SEO strategy. Your SEO strategy should align with your overall business goals and define the tactics you will use to achieve your SEO objectives.

2. Conduct Keyword Research

Keyword research is a critical component of SEO, as it enables you to identify the keywords your target audience is searching for and optimize your website accordingly. Keyword research involves analyzing the search volume, competition, and relevance of keywords related to your business.

3. Analyze Your Website

Before you can optimize your website for search engines, you need to analyze your website's current performance. This involves analyzing your website's content, structure, and technical performance.

4. Develop a Content Strategy

Developing a content strategy is essential for optimizing your website for search engines. Your content strategy should identify the topics and keywords you will target with your content, the types of content you will create, and the channels you will use to promote your content.

5. Implement On-Page Optimization

On-page optimization involves optimizing your website's content, structure, and HTML code to improve its visibility to search engines. This includes optimizing your website's title tags, meta descriptions, headers, and internal linking structure.

6. Build Backlinks

Backlinks are a critical component of SEO, as they signal to search engines that other websites find your content valuable and relevant. Building high-quality backlinks involves creating valuable content that other websites will want to link to, as well as reaching out to other websites to request backlinks.

7. Monitor and Adjust Your SEO Strategy

SEO is an ongoing process, and it is essential to monitor and adjust your SEO strategy regularly. This involves tracking your website's performance using SEO KPIs and adjusting your strategy as needed to achieve your SEO objectives.

Conclusion

Setting up a programmatic SEO framework involves defining your SEO strategy, conducting keyword research, analyzing your website, developing a content strategy, implementing on-page optimization, building backlinks, and monitoring and adjusting your SEO strategy. By following these steps, you can optimize your website for search engines and achieve your desired SEO outcomes.

Chapter 7: Allocating Budget and Resources for Programmatic SEO

Allocating budget and resources for programmatic SEO is essential for implementing and maintaining an effective SEO strategy. In this chapter, we will explore the process of allocating budget and resources for programmatic SEO.

1. Determine Your Budget

The first step in allocating budget for programmatic SEO is to determine how much you can afford to spend. Your SEO budget should be based on the resources available to you and the goals you want to achieve with your SEO efforts.

2. Prioritize SEO Tasks

Once you have determined your SEO budget, the next step is to prioritize SEO tasks based on their importance and the resources required to complete them. Prioritizing SEO tasks can help you allocate your resources more effectively and ensure that you are focusing on the most important tasks.

3. Allocate Resources

After prioritizing SEO tasks, the next step is to allocate resources to each task. Resources may include staff time, third-party tools, or external contractors. Allocating resources effectively can help you complete SEO tasks efficiently and within your budget.

4. Monitor and Adjust Resource Allocation

As your SEO strategy evolves, it is essential to monitor and adjust your resource allocation accordingly. This may involve reallocating resources from lower-priority tasks to higher-priority tasks or increasing your SEO budget to achieve your desired outcomes.

5. Measure ROI

Measuring the return on investment (ROI) of your programmatic SEO efforts is essential for justifying your SEO budget and demonstrating the value of your SEO strategy. By tracking key performance indicators (KPIs) and measuring the ROI of your SEO efforts, you can optimize your budget and ensure that your SEO strategy is delivering measurable results.

Conclusion
Allocating budget and resources for programmatic SEO involves determining your SEO budget, prioritizing SEO tasks, allocating resources, monitoring and adjusting resource allocation, and measuring ROI. By following these steps, you can optimize your SEO budget and resources and achieve your desired SEO outcomes.

Chapter 8: Keyword Research and Mapping

Keyword research and mapping are critical components of programmatic SEO, as they enable you to identify the keywords your target audience is searching for and optimize your website accordingly. In this chapter, we will explore the process of keyword research and mapping.

Define Your SEO Objectives
The first step in conducting keyword research and mapping is to define your SEO objectives. Your SEO objectives should align with your overall business goals and define the keywords you will target with your SEO efforts.

Identify Seed Keywords
Seed keywords are the basic building blocks of your keyword research. They are broad, general keywords related to your business or industry that you can use to generate more specific, targeted keywords. Identify a list of seed keywords that are relevant to your business or industry.

Use Keyword Research Tools
Keyword research tools can help you generate a comprehensive list of keywords related to your business or industry. These tools allow you to analyze search volume, competition, and relevance for each keyword.

Analyze Your Competitors' Keywords
Analyzing your competitors' keywords can provide valuable insights into the keywords they are targeting and how you can optimize your website to compete effectively. Use competitor analysis tools to analyze your competitors' keywords.

Map Keywords to Pages

Once you have identified your target keywords, the next step is to map them to the pages on your website. Keyword mapping involves assigning each keyword to a specific page on your website and optimizing that page accordingly.

Optimize On-Page Elements
On-page optimization involves optimizing your website's content, structure, and HTML code to improve its visibility to search engines. This includes optimizing your website's title tags, meta descriptions, headers, and internal linking structure.

Create Content Based on Keywords
Creating content based on your target keywords can help you improve your website's relevance to those keywords and improve its visibility in search engine results. Create high-quality, engaging content that incorporates your target keywords naturally.

Conclusion

Keyword research and mapping are essential components of programmatic SEO. By identifying your target keywords, mapping them to your website pages, and optimizing your website accordingly, you can improve your website's visibility to search engines and attract more targeted traffic to your website. By following these steps, you can optimize your keyword research and mapping process and achieve your desired SEO outcomes.

Chapter 9: Content optimization and generation

Content optimization and generation are critical components of programmatic SEO, as they enable you to create high-quality, engaging content that appeals to your target audience and improves your website's visibility in search engine results. In this chapter, we will explore the process of content optimization and generation.

1. Identify Your Target Audience

The first step in optimizing and generating content is to identify your target audience. Your content should be tailored to the needs and interests of your target audience, as this will increase engagement and improve your website's visibility in search engine results.

2. Conduct Keyword Research

Keyword research is essential for identifying the keywords and topics your target audience is searching for. Use keyword research tools to identify relevant keywords and topics and incorporate them into your content strategy.

3. Optimize On-Page Elements

On-page optimization involves optimizing your website's content, structure, and HTML code to improve its visibility to search engines. This includes optimizing your website's title tags, meta descriptions, headers, and internal linking structure.

4. Create High-Quality Content

Creating high-quality content is essential for engaging your target audience and improving your website's visibility in search engine results. Focus on creating content that is informative, engaging, and valuable to your target audience.

5. Incorporate Multimedia Elements

Incorporating multimedia elements into your content can help improve engagement and increase your website's visibility in search engine results. This includes incorporating images, videos, infographics, and other visual elements into your content.

6. Optimize for User Experience

Optimizing your content for user experience is essential for improving engagement and increasing your website's visibility in search engine results. This includes ensuring that your website is mobile-friendly, easy to navigate, and loads quickly.

7. Monitor and Analyze Content Performance

Monitoring and analyzing your content's performance can help you identify areas for improvement and optimize your content strategy accordingly. Use analytics tools to track metrics such as page views, bounce rates, and time on page.

Conclusion

Content optimization and generation are essential components of programmatic SEO. By identifying your target audience, conducting keyword research, optimizing on-page elements, creating high-quality content, incorporating multimedia elements, optimizing for user experience, and monitoring and analyzing content performance, you can improve your website's visibility in search engine results and attract more targeted traffic to your website. By following these steps, you can optimize your content optimization and generation process and achieve your desired SEO outcomes.

Chapter 10: Link building and outreach

Link building is a crucial component of programmatic SEO as it helps improve your website's authority and visibility in search engine results. In this chapter, we will explore the process of link building and outreach.

1. Identify Link Building Opportunities

The first step in link building is to identify opportunities for acquiring high-quality backlinks. This can be done by conducting competitor research, exploring broken link building opportunities, and building relationships with other relevant websites.

2. Develop Linkable Assets

Linkable assets are high-quality content pieces that can be used to attract backlinks from other websites. These can include infographics, guides, whitepapers, and other types of content that are relevant and valuable to your target audience.

3. Outreach to Relevant Websites

Outreach to relevant websites is an essential component of link building. This involves reaching out to website owners and influencers to promote your linkable assets and acquire backlinks.

4. Guest Blogging

Guest blogging involves writing blog posts for other websites in exchange for a backlink to your website. This can be an effective way to acquire high-quality backlinks and increase your website's authority.

5. Monitor and Analyze Link Performance

Monitoring and analyzing your backlink profile is essential for identifying areas for improvement and optimizing your link building strategy. Use backlink analysis tools to track your backlink profile and identify areas for improvement.

Conclusion

Link building and outreach are critical components of programmatic SEO, as they help improve your website's authority and visibility in search engine results. By identifying link building opportunities, developing linkable assets, reaching out to relevant websites, guest blogging, and monitoring and analyzing link performance, you can improve your website's backlink profile and achieve your desired SEO outcomes. By following these steps, you can optimize your link building and outreach process and achieve sustainable SEO success.

Chapter 11: On-page and technical SEO

On-page and technical SEO are critical components of programmatic SEO, as they help improve your website's relevance, usability, and search engine friendliness. In this chapter, we will explore the process of on-page and technical SEO.

1. Conduct a Technical SEO Audit

The first step in technical SEO is to conduct a comprehensive audit of your website's technical infrastructure. This includes assessing your website's crawlability, indexability, site speed, and mobile-friendliness.

2. Optimize On-Page Elements

On-page optimization involves optimizing individual web pages to improve their relevance and search engine friendliness. This includes optimizing title tags, meta descriptions, header tags, content, and internal linking.

3. Optimize for User Experience

User experience optimization involves optimizing your website to improve its usability, accessibility, and user engagement. This includes optimizing site architecture, navigation, site search, and mobile-friendliness.

4. Ensure Secure and Accessible Website

Secure and accessible website means a website that is safe to use and easily accessible by all types of users. This includes implementing HTTPS, ensuring compliance with web accessibility standards, and optimizing for mobile devices.

5. Monitor and Analyze Technical SEO Performance

Monitoring and analyzing your website's technical SEO performance is essential for identifying areas for improvement and optimizing your technical SEO strategy. Use technical SEO tools to track your website's technical SEO health and identify areas for improvement.

Conclusion

On-page and technical SEO are essential components of programmatic SEO, as they help improve your website's relevance, usability, and search engine friendliness. By conducting a technical SEO audit, optimizing on-page elements, optimizing for user experience, ensuring secure and accessible website, and monitoring and analyzing technical SEO performance, you can improve your website's technical infrastructure and achieve your desired SEO outcomes. By following these steps, you can optimize your on-page and technical SEO process and achieve sustainable SEO success.

Chapter 12: Analytics and reporting

Analytics and reporting are critical components of programmatic SEO, as they help track your website's performance, measure the effectiveness of your SEO strategies, and identify areas for improvement. In this chapter, we will explore the process of analytics and reporting.

1. Set Up Analytics Tools

The first step in analytics and reporting is to set up analytics tools to track your website's performance. Google Analytics is a popular tool for tracking website traffic, user behavior, and conversions.

2. Define SEO Metrics and KPIs

Define SEO metrics and KPIs that align with your SEO objectives and goals. These metrics can include website traffic, user engagement, conversion rates, and search engine rankings.

3. Create Custom Reports

Custom reports can help you track your SEO performance and identify areas for improvement. Use analytics tools to create custom reports that track your defined SEO metrics and KPIs.

4. Monitor and Analyze Performance

Monitoring and analyzing your website's performance is essential for identifying areas for improvement and optimizing your SEO strategies. Use analytics tools to track your website's performance over time and identify areas for improvement.

5. Continuously Optimize SEO Strategies

Continuously optimize your SEO strategies based on your analytics and reporting data. Use your data to identify areas for improvement, adjust your SEO strategies, and achieve your desired SEO outcomes.

Conclusion

Analytics and reporting are essential components of programmatic SEO, as they help track your website's performance, measure the effectiveness of your SEO strategies, and identify areas for improvement. By setting up analytics tools, defining SEO metrics and KPIs, creating custom reports, monitoring and analyzing performance, and continuously optimizing SEO strategies, you can achieve sustainable SEO success. By following these steps, you can optimize your analytics and reporting process and achieve your desired SEO outcomes.

Chapter 13: Cross-channel integration strategies

Cross-channel integration is a critical component of programmatic SEO, as it helps create a cohesive and consistent online presence and increase the effectiveness of your SEO strategies. In this chapter, we will explore the process of cross-channel integration strategies.

1. Integrate SEO with Other Digital Marketing Channels
Integrate your SEO strategies with other digital marketing channels, such as social media, content marketing, email marketing, and paid search. This can help increase your website's visibility, drive traffic, and improve your overall online presence.

2. Leverage Data from Other Channels
Leverage data from other digital marketing channels to inform your SEO strategies. Use data from social media, content marketing, email marketing, and paid search to identify keywords, content ideas, and user behavior insights.

3. Optimize for Mobile Devices
Optimize your website for mobile devices, as more and more users are accessing websites through mobile devices. This includes optimizing site speed, mobile-friendly design, and mobile-first indexing.

4. Use Local SEO Strategies
Use local SEO strategies to target local audiences and improve your website's visibility in local search results. This includes optimizing your Google My Business listing, creating local content, and building local citations.

5. Monitor and Analyze Cross-Channel Performance
Monitor and analyze your cross-channel performance to identify areas for improvement and optimize your cross-channel integration strategies. Use analytics tools to track your website's performance across different digital marketing channels.

Conclusion

Cross-channel integration is essential for achieving sustainable SEO success, as it helps create a cohesive and consistent online presence and increase the effectiveness of your SEO strategies. By integrating SEO with other digital marketing channels, leveraging data from other channels, optimizing for mobile devices, using local SEO strategies, and monitoring and analyzing cross-channel performance, you can achieve your desired SEO outcomes. By following these steps, you can optimize your cross-channel integration process and achieve sustainable SEO success.

Chapter 14: SEO and PPC: An integrated approach

SEO and PPC are two different digital marketing channels that often operate separately. However, by integrating the two, you can achieve even greater results. In this chapter, we will explore how to integrate SEO and PPC for an effective digital marketing strategy.

1. Understanding the Differences Between SEO and PPC

SEO is a long-term strategy that involves optimizing your website to improve its organic search rankings. PPC, on the other hand, is a paid advertising strategy that involves placing ads in search engine results pages (SERPs).

2. Benefits of Integrating SEO and PPC

Integrating SEO and PPC offers several benefits, such as:

- Increased visibility in SERPs
- Greater control over your search engine presence
- Improved keyword targeting
- Enhanced customer insights
- Improved conversion rates

3. Developing an Integrated SEO and PPC Strategy

To develop an integrated SEO and PPC strategy, follow these steps:

- Identify keywords that are performing well in both SEO and PPC.
- Optimize your landing pages to align with your PPC ads and improve your SEO performance.
- Use PPC ads to test new keywords and assess their performance before investing in long-term SEO strategies.
- Use SEO data to inform your PPC ad targeting and bidding strategies.
- Analyze your data from both SEO and PPC to identify areas for improvement and adjust your strategies accordingly.

4. Best Practices for SEO and PPC Integration

To ensure the success of your integrated SEO and PPC strategy, follow these best practices:

- Set clear goals and KPIs for both SEO and PPC.
- Align your messaging and branding across both channels.
- Coordinate your keyword strategies to avoid competing with yourself in search engine results.
- Use data and analytics to continuously refine your strategies.

Conclusion

Integrating SEO and PPC is an effective way to maximize the benefits of both channels and achieve greater results. By understanding the differences between SEO and PPC, developing an integrated strategy, and following best practices, you can improve your visibility in SERPs, increase your control over your search engine presence, and enhance your overall digital marketing performance.

Chapter 15: Programmatic SEO and social media marketing

Social media marketing is a crucial component of any digital marketing strategy, and integrating it with programmatic SEO can lead to even greater results. In this chapter, we will explore how programmatic SEO and social media marketing can work together to enhance your overall digital marketing performance.

1. Understanding the Benefits of Social Media Marketing
Social media marketing involves using social media platforms to promote your brand, products, or services. The benefits of social media marketing include:
- Increased brand awareness
- Improved customer engagement
- Enhanced customer insights
- Greater control over your online reputation
- Improved conversion rates

2. Benefits of Integrating Programmatic SEO and Social Media Marketing
Integrating programmatic SEO and social media marketing can offer several benefits, such as:
- Improved search engine rankings
- Increased traffic to your website
- Greater control over your online presence
- Improved customer engagement
- Enhanced customer insights

3. Developing an Integrated Programmatic SEO and Social Media Marketing Strategy
To develop an integrated programmatic SEO and social media marketing strategy, follow these steps:
- Use social media to promote your content and drive traffic to your website.
- Use social media to engage with your customers and build relationships.

- Use programmatic SEO to optimize your website for search engines and improve your organic search rankings.
- Use programmatic SEO data to inform your social media marketing strategy, such as by identifying popular keywords and topics to target.
- Analyze your data from both programmatic SEO and social media to identify areas for improvement and adjust your strategies accordingly.
4. Best Practices for Integrating Programmatic SEO and Social Media Marketing

To ensure the success of your integrated programmatic SEO and social media marketing strategy, follow these best practices:

- Set clear goals and KPIs for both programmatic SEO and social media marketing.
- Coordinate your messaging and branding across both channels.
- Use programmatic SEO data to inform your social media targeting and messaging strategies.
- Use social media data to inform your programmatic SEO keyword and content strategies.
- Continuously analyze and refine your data to optimize your strategies.

Conclusion

Integrating programmatic SEO and social media marketing can lead to even greater results for your digital marketing strategy. By understanding the benefits of social media marketing, developing an integrated strategy, and following best practices, you can improve your search engine rankings, increase your website traffic, enhance your customer engagement, and ultimately, achieve greater digital marketing success.

Chapter 16: Programmatic SEO and email marketing

Email marketing is a highly effective digital marketing tactic that involves sending promotional messages to a targeted audience via email. Integrating programmatic SEO with email marketing can help to optimize your email campaigns, improve your email deliverability, and increase your email open and click-through rates. In this chapter, we will explore how programmatic SEO and email marketing can work together to enhance your overall digital marketing performance.

1. Understanding the Benefits of Email Marketing

Email marketing is a powerful tool for businesses, offering several benefits such as:

- Building brand loyalty and trust
- Generating leads and sales
- Increasing website traffic
- Providing a direct and personal way to communicate with your audience

2. Benefits of Integrating Programmatic SEO and Email Marketing

Integrating programmatic SEO and email marketing can offer several benefits, such as:

- Improved email deliverability
- Higher open and click-through rates
- Better audience targeting
- Increased lead generation and conversion rates
- Improved search engine rankings

3. Developing an Integrated Programmatic SEO and Email Marketing Strategy

To develop an integrated programmatic SEO and email marketing strategy, follow these steps:

- Use programmatic SEO to optimize your website content for specific keywords and phrases that your target audience is searching for.

- Use programmatic SEO data to inform your email marketing strategy, such as by identifying popular keywords and topics to target in your email campaigns.
- Use email marketing to promote your website content and drive traffic to your site.
- Use email marketing to engage with your audience and build relationships.
- Analyze your data from both programmatic SEO and email marketing to identify areas for improvement and adjust your strategies accordingly.
4. Best Practices for Integrating Programmatic SEO and Email Marketing

To ensure the success of your integrated programmatic SEO and email marketing strategy, follow these best practices:

- Segment your email list based on interests and behaviors to improve targeting and engagement.
- Use programmatic SEO data to inform your email subject lines, content, and CTAs.
- Use email marketing to promote your website content and drive traffic to your site.
- Optimize your website landing pages to align with your email marketing campaigns.
- Continuously analyze and refine your data to optimize your strategies.

Conclusion

Integrating programmatic SEO and email marketing can lead to even greater results for your digital marketing strategy. By understanding the benefits of email marketing, developing an integrated strategy, and following best practices, you can improve your email deliverability, increase your open and click-through rates, enhance your audience targeting and engagement, and ultimately, achieve greater digital marketing success.

Chapter 17: SEO automation tools and software

SEO automation tools and software can help businesses streamline their SEO processes, save time and resources, and improve their overall SEO performance. In this chapter, we will explore the different types of SEO automation tools and software available and their benefits.

1. Types of SEO Automation Tools and Software

There are several types of SEO automation tools and software available, including:

- Keyword research and analysis tools
- On-page optimization tools
- Backlink analysis and monitoring tools
- Reporting and analytics tools
- Technical SEO tools
- Content optimization and generation tools
- Local SEO tools
- E-commerce SEO tools

2. Benefits of SEO Automation Tools and Software

Using SEO automation tools and software can offer several benefits, including:

- Saving time and resources
- Reducing human error
- Improving accuracy and consistency
- Scaling SEO efforts
- Providing data-driven insights for decision-making
- Increasing productivity and efficiency
- Improving ROI

3. Choosing the Right SEO Automation Tools and Software

To choose the right SEO automation tools and software, consider the following factors:

- Your specific SEO goals and objectives
- The size of your business and SEO team
- The complexity of your SEO strategy
- Your budget and resources

- The level of automation you want to achieve
- The ease of use and compatibility with your existing tools and software

4. Top SEO Automation Tools and Software

Some of the top SEO automation tools and software include:

- SEMrush
- Ahrefs
- Moz
- Google Analytics
- Google Search Console
- Yoast SEO
- Screaming Frog
- HubSpot
- BrightLocal
- Majestic SEO

5. Using SEO Automation Tools and Software Effectively

To use SEO automation tools and software effectively, follow these best practices:

- Choose the right tools and software for your business and goals
- Integrate your tools and software for maximum efficiency
- Continuously monitor and analyze your data for insights and improvements
- Regularly review and update your SEO strategy based on your data and results
- Train your team on how to use the tools and software effectively

Conclusion

SEO automation tools and software can help businesses improve their SEO performance, save time and resources, and achieve greater success. By understanding the different types of tools available, their benefits, and how to choose and use them effectively, businesses can take their SEO strategy to the next level and achieve greater ROI.

Chapter 18: Data science tools for SEO

Data science tools are becoming increasingly important for businesses looking to improve their SEO performance. In this chapter, we will explore the different types of data science tools available for SEO and their benefits.

1. Types of Data Science Tools for SEO

There are several types of data science tools available for SEO, including:

- Predictive analytics tools
- Machine learning algorithms
- Natural language processing (NLP) tools
- Data visualization tools
- Clustering and classification tools
- Sentiment analysis tools
- Deep learning tools
- Recommendation engines

2. Benefits of Data Science Tools for SEO

Using data science tools for SEO can offer several benefits, including:

- Improving keyword research and analysis
- Enhancing content optimization and generation
- Improving backlink analysis and monitoring
- Enhancing user experience and engagement
- Optimizing for voice search and natural language queries
- Providing data-driven insights for decision-making
- Improving ROI

3. Choosing the Right Data Science Tools for SEO

To choose the right data science tools for SEO, consider the following factors:

- Your specific SEO goals and objectives
- The size of your business and SEO team
- The complexity of your SEO strategy
- Your budget and resources
- The level of automation you want to achieve

- The ease of use and compatibility with your existing tools and software
4. Top Data Science Tools for SEO

Some of the top data science tools for SEO include:

- Google Cloud AI Platform
- IBM Watson Studio
- Microsoft Azure Machine Learning
- TensorFlow
- Python
- Tableau
- RapidMiner
- Hadoop
- Apache Spark
- BigML

5. Using Data Science Tools for SEO Effectively

To use data science tools for SEO effectively, follow these best practices:

- Choose the right tools and software for your business and goals
- Ensure your data is accurate and relevant
- Continuously monitor and analyze your data for insights and improvements
- Regularly review and update your SEO strategy based on your data and results
- Train your team on how to use the tools and software effectively

Conclusion

Data science tools for SEO can help businesses improve their SEO performance, provide data-driven insights, and achieve greater success. By understanding the different types of tools available, their benefits, and how to choose and use them effectively, businesses can take their SEO strategy to the next level and achieve greater ROI.

Chapter 19: Keyword research tools

Keyword research is a crucial component of any successful SEO strategy. In this chapter, we will explore the different types of keyword research tools available and their benefits.

1. Types of Keyword Research Tools

There are several types of keyword research tools available, including:

- Keyword planners: These tools provide insights into the search volume, competition, and suggested bid for specific keywords. Examples include Google Keyword Planner, Moz Keyword Explorer, and Ahrefs Keywords Explorer.
- Competitor analysis tools: These tools help you identify the keywords your competitors are ranking for and the strategies they are using. Examples include SEMrush and SpyFu.
- Topic research tools: These tools help you discover new content ideas and related keywords based on a topic or keyword. Examples include Answer the Public and BuzzSumo.
- Keyword suggestion tools: These tools provide suggestions for related or long-tail keywords based on a seed keyword. Examples include Ubersuggest and KeywordTool.io.
- Analytics tools: These tools help you analyze your website's current keyword performance and identify opportunities for improvement. Examples include Google Analytics and Search Console.

2. Benefits of Keyword Research Tools

Using keyword research tools can offer several benefits, including:

- Finding new and relevant keywords to target
- Discovering search trends and patterns
- Identifying keyword opportunities for content creation and optimization

- Understanding your audience and their search behavior
- Optimizing for voice search and natural language queries
- Improving your overall SEO strategy and performance
3. Choosing the Right Keyword Research Tools

To choose the right keyword research tools, consider the following factors:

- Your specific SEO goals and objectives
- The size of your business and SEO team
- The complexity of your SEO strategy
- Your budget and resources
- The level of automation you want to achieve
- The ease of use and compatibility with your existing tools and software
4. Top Keyword Research Tools

Some of the top keyword research tools include:

- Google Keyword Planner
- Moz Keyword Explorer
- SEMrush
- Ahrefs Keywords Explorer
- Answer the Public
- Ubersuggest
- KeywordTool.io
- SpyFu
- BuzzSumo
5. Using Keyword Research Tools Effectively

To use keyword research tools effectively, follow these best practices:

- Set clear goals and objectives for your keyword research
- Use multiple tools to get a comprehensive view of your keywords and opportunities
- Use data-driven insights to inform your content creation and optimization strategy

- Continuously monitor and analyze your keyword performance and adjust your strategy as needed
- Don't rely solely on keyword volume and competition metrics, also consider the relevance and intent of the keywords.

Conclusion

Keyword research tools are essential for any successful SEO strategy. By understanding the different types of tools available, their benefits, and how to choose and use them effectively, businesses can optimize their content, improve their rankings, and achieve greater success.

Chapter 20: Analytics and reporting tools

One of the key aspects of programmatic SEO is the ability to track and analyze data effectively. Analytics and reporting tools play a crucial role in this regard, as they provide insights into the performance of various SEO campaigns and help marketers optimize their strategies accordingly. In this chapter, we will discuss some of the most popular analytics and reporting tools used in programmatic SEO.

1. Google Analytics: Google Analytics is a free web analytics service offered by Google. It provides valuable insights into website traffic and user behavior, allowing marketers to track key metrics such as pageviews, bounce rates, and time on site. In addition to this, Google Analytics also offers a range of customization options, including the ability to set up goals and funnels, track conversions, and segment data by various dimensions.

2. SEMrush: SEMrush is an all-in-one SEO tool that offers a range of features, including keyword research, site audits, and competitor analysis. One of its key features is its ability to track and report on keyword rankings over time. SEMrush also offers a range of analytics and reporting tools, including the ability to track backlinks, analyze organic search traffic, and identify content gaps.

3. Ahrefs: Ahrefs is another popular SEO tool that offers a range of features, including keyword research, site audits, and competitor analysis. Ahrefs' reporting tools provide insights into organic search traffic, backlinks, and keyword rankings. It also offers a content explorer tool that allows marketers to identify popular content in their niche and track its performance over time.

4. Moz Pro: Moz Pro is a suite of SEO tools that includes features such as keyword research, site audits, and link analysis. Moz Pro also offers a range of reporting options, including the ability to track keyword rankings, analyze link data, and monitor site performance over time. Moz Pro also offers a proprietary metric called Domain Authority, which is used to evaluate the overall authority of a website in search engine rankings.

5. Raven Tools: Raven Tools is an all-in-one SEO tool that offers features such as keyword research, site audits, and backlink analysis. Its reporting tools provide insights into organic search traffic, keyword rankings, and link data. Raven Tools also offers the ability to create custom reports that can be white-labeled and exported in a variety of formats.

In conclusion, analytics and reporting tools are essential for programmatic SEO. These tools allow marketers to track and analyze data effectively, providing insights into the performance of various SEO campaigns and helping to optimize strategies accordingly. While there are many analytics and reporting tools available, the ones discussed in this chapter are some of the most popular and widely used in the industry.

Chapter 21: Successful programmatic SEO implementation stories

Programmatic SEO has revolutionized the way businesses approach search engine optimization. By automating several tasks and utilizing data-driven strategies, programmatic SEO has enabled businesses to achieve better results in less time. Many businesses have implemented programmatic SEO, and the success stories of such businesses provide valuable insights into how programmatic SEO can benefit businesses. Here are some successful programmatic SEO implementation stories:

1. Airbnb

Airbnb is a popular online marketplace that connects travelers with hosts who have extra space to rent. Airbnb implemented programmatic SEO to increase its visibility on search engines and to drive more traffic to its website. The programmatic SEO strategy involved identifying the right keywords and optimizing the content for those keywords. The programmatic SEO implementation resulted in a 30% increase in organic traffic and a significant increase in the number of bookings.

2. Casper

Casper is a popular online mattress retailer. Casper implemented programmatic SEO to improve its organic search rankings and to drive more traffic to its website. The programmatic SEO strategy involved optimizing the website structure, improving the content quality, and leveraging data to identify the right keywords to target. The programmatic SEO implementation resulted in a 50% increase in organic traffic and a significant increase in revenue.

3. Warby Parker

Warby Parker is an online eyewear retailer. Warby Parker implemented programmatic SEO to improve its visibility on search engines and to drive more traffic to its website. The programmatic SEO strategy involved improving the website structure, creating high-quality content, and leveraging data to identify the right keywords to target. The programmatic SEO implementation resulted in a 40% increase in organic traffic and a significant increase in revenue.

4. HubSpot

HubSpot is a leading inbound marketing and sales software company. HubSpot implemented programmatic SEO to improve its visibility on search engines and to drive more traffic to its website. The programmatic SEO strategy involved creating high-quality content, optimizing the website structure, and leveraging data to identify the right keywords to target. The programmatic SEO implementation resulted in a 30% increase in organic traffic and a significant increase in revenue.

These successful programmatic SEO implementation stories demonstrate how programmatic SEO can help businesses achieve their SEO objectives and drive more traffic to their website. By leveraging data-driven strategies, businesses can optimize their website and content for the right keywords and improve their visibility on search engines. Programmatic SEO implementation can result in a significant increase in organic traffic, revenue, and customer acquisition.

Chapter 22: Challenges and lessons learned

Implementing programmatic SEO can be a complex and challenging process, and there are several common obstacles that organizations may encounter. In this chapter, we will discuss some of the main challenges that businesses face when implementing programmatic SEO and offer some lessons learned to help overcome these hurdles.

1. Lack of Resources: One of the primary challenges of implementing programmatic SEO is the need for dedicated resources. While automation tools can streamline some aspects of SEO, the process still requires significant time and effort to execute effectively. Businesses must invest in skilled professionals or agency partners to manage programmatic SEO campaigns successfully.

2. Complexity of Automation Tools: Automation tools can be highly complex and require specialized skills to operate. Without proper training, businesses may struggle to utilize these tools to their full potential.

3. Misalignment with Business Goals: Another common challenge is misalignment between programmatic SEO goals and broader business objectives. When SEO is seen as a standalone activity rather than a strategic part of the marketing mix, businesses may struggle to see the value in programmatic SEO and may not allocate the necessary resources to the effort.

4. Fluctuating Algorithm Changes: Google's algorithms are continually evolving, which means that businesses must stay up-to-date on changes and adapt their programmatic SEO strategies accordingly. Algorithm updates can significantly impact the visibility and ranking of websites and can pose a challenge for businesses that are not keeping up.

Lessons Learned:

1. Start Small: Businesses should start with a small pilot programmatic SEO program and focus on optimizing key landing pages. This approach allows organizations to test the effectiveness of automation tools and identify potential roadblocks before expanding to a more extensive campaign.
2. Align SEO Goals with Business Goals: Businesses must align SEO goals with broader business objectives and develop KPIs that reflect this alignment. This approach ensures that programmatic SEO is seen as a strategic part of the marketing mix, rather than a standalone activity.
3. Invest in Skilled Professionals: It is essential to invest in skilled professionals or agency partners with experience in programmatic SEO. This investment can provide valuable insights and ensure that automation tools are being used to their full potential.
4. Stay Up-to-Date: Businesses must stay up-to-date on algorithm updates and adapt their programmatic SEO strategies accordingly. This approach ensures that organizations remain competitive and continue to achieve desired results.

In conclusion, programmatic SEO implementation can be a challenging process, but businesses can overcome these obstacles by starting small, aligning SEO goals with business objectives, investing in skilled professionals, and staying up-to-date on algorithm changes. By following these lessons learned, organizations can successfully implement programmatic SEO and achieve their desired results.

Chapter 23: Future trends in programmatic SEO

Programmatic SEO is a constantly evolving field, and as technology advances, new trends emerge that shape the way we optimize websites for search engines. In this chapter, we'll explore some of the emerging trends in programmatic SEO and what they could mean for the future of the field.

1. Voice search optimization: With the increasing popularity of voice assistants like Amazon's Alexa and Google Home, voice search is quickly becoming a dominant way people search for information online. Programmatic SEO will need to adapt to this trend by optimizing websites for voice search queries, which often differ from traditional text-based searches.

2. Artificial intelligence (AI) and machine learning: AI and machine learning are already being used in programmatic SEO, but their role is likely to become even more significant in the future. With the help of AI, SEO professionals can analyze large amounts of data and make informed decisions about how to optimize their websites.

3. Predictive analytics: Predictive analytics is a field of data analytics that uses statistical algorithms and machine learning techniques to predict future outcomes based on historical data. In programmatic SEO, predictive analytics can be used to identify patterns and trends in user behavior, allowing SEO professionals to make more informed decisions about how to optimize their websites.

4. Visual search optimization: Visual search is another emerging trend in programmatic SEO, with tools like Google Lens and Pinterest Lens allowing users to search for information using images instead of text. SEO professionals will need to adapt to this trend by optimizing their websites for visual search queries.

5. Local SEO: With the rise of mobile devices and location-based services, local SEO has become increasingly important for businesses that want to reach customers in their area. Programmatic SEO will need to adapt to this trend by optimizing websites for local search queries, including the use of location-specific keywords and schema markup.
6. Data privacy and security: With data breaches and privacy concerns becoming more common, data privacy and security will become increasingly important in programmatic SEO. SEO professionals will need to ensure that they are using secure tools and following best practices for data protection.
7. User experience optimization: User experience (UX) has always been an important factor in SEO, but it will become even more critical in the future. SEO professionals will need to focus on optimizing their websites for a seamless user experience across devices and platforms, including fast loading times, intuitive navigation, and mobile responsiveness.

In conclusion, programmatic SEO is an ever-changing field that requires SEO professionals to stay up-to-date with emerging trends and technologies. By adapting to these trends and embracing new tools and techniques, SEO professionals can stay ahead of the competition and ensure that their websites remain optimized for search engines in the future.

Chapter 24: The potential of programmatic SEO in transforming digital marketing

Programmatic SEO is a rapidly growing field, and its potential for transforming digital marketing is significant. As search engines and user behavior continue to evolve, programmatic SEO provides businesses with the tools and insights they need to stay ahead of the curve.

One of the key benefits of programmatic SEO is its ability to provide highly targeted and personalized search experiences. With the right tools and techniques, businesses can use programmatic SEO to deliver highly relevant content and messaging to individual users, based on their search history, demographics, and other data points. This can lead to higher engagement, more conversions, and stronger brand loyalty over time.

Another potential benefit of programmatic SEO is its ability to drive greater efficiency and cost-effectiveness in digital marketing. By automating many of the time-consuming and repetitive tasks associated with SEO, businesses can save significant amounts of time and resources, allowing them to focus on more strategic activities like content creation, outreach, and analytics.

At the same time, programmatic SEO can also help businesses stay up-to-date with the latest trends and best practices in SEO. By leveraging data-driven insights and machine learning algorithms, businesses can gain a deeper understanding of how search engines are evolving, and adjust their strategies accordingly. This can help them stay ahead of the curve and achieve better results over time.

Overall, programmatic SEO has the potential to transform digital marketing in a variety of ways. By providing businesses with the tools and insights they need to optimize their search strategies and stay ahead of the curve, programmatic SEO can help drive greater engagement, conversions, and brand loyalty over time. As the field continues to evolve, it is likely that we will see even more powerful and innovative applications of programmatic SEO in the years to come.

Chapter 25: Key takeaways and action points for marketers

Programmatic SEO is a complex and rapidly evolving field, but there are a few key takeaways and action points that marketers can keep in mind as they develop their own strategies and approaches.

First, it is important to recognize that programmatic SEO is not a one-size-fits-all solution. Every business is different, and every SEO strategy must be tailored to the unique needs and goals of the organization. This means that businesses should be prepared to invest in the right tools, resources, and expertise to develop and implement a successful programmatic SEO strategy.

Second, marketers should be aware of the potential benefits and challenges associated with programmatic SEO. On the one hand, programmatic SEO can help drive greater efficiency, cost-effectiveness, and user engagement in digital marketing. On the other hand, it can be difficult to implement and optimize, and may require ongoing investments in technology, training, and personnel to achieve the desired results.

Third, businesses should focus on developing a strong data-driven approach to programmatic SEO. This means leveraging tools and technologies that can help them collect, analyze, and interpret data from a variety of sources, including search engines, social media, and web analytics. By using data-driven insights to inform their SEO strategies, businesses can stay ahead of the curve and achieve better results over time.

Fourth, it is important to maintain a holistic approach to SEO, focusing not just on keywords and rankings, but on the overall user experience. This means investing in high-quality content, user-friendly design, and responsive customer service, in addition to traditional SEO techniques like keyword research and link building.

Finally, businesses should be prepared to experiment and iterate as they develop and refine their programmatic SEO strategies. SEO is a constantly evolving field, and what works today may not work tomorrow. By remaining open to new ideas, testing new approaches, and adapting to changing market conditions, businesses can stay ahead of the curve and achieve long-term success in programmatic SEO.

In summary, programmatic SEO has the potential to transform digital marketing, but it requires a thoughtful and strategic approach. By focusing on data-driven insights, holistic user experiences, and ongoing experimentation and iteration, marketers can develop and implement successful programmatic SEO strategies that drive engagement, conversions, and brand loyalty over time.

Chapter 26: Final thoughts on programmatic SEO as a game-changer in SEO optimization

Programmatic SEO has rapidly become an indispensable tool for any marketer looking to optimize their website for search engines. This innovative approach to SEO optimization offers numerous benefits, including increased efficiency, scalability, and data-driven decision making.

In this book, we have explored the historical evolution of SEO automation, the current state of programmatic SEO, and its future trends. We have examined the key components of a successful programmatic SEO strategy, including keyword research, content optimization, link building, technical SEO, analytics, and cross-channel integration. We have also highlighted the importance of using data science tools and automation software to streamline and enhance SEO processes.

As we conclude this book, it is clear that programmatic SEO is transforming the digital marketing landscape. By leveraging the power of automation and data analysis, marketers can not only achieve higher search engine rankings but also gain valuable insights into user behavior and preferences. This, in turn, can help them create more targeted and effective marketing campaigns, leading to increased customer engagement, retention, and sales.

In summary, programmatic SEO is a game-changer in SEO optimization. It offers numerous benefits, challenges, and opportunities for marketers to transform their digital marketing strategies. As such, it is essential that marketers stay up-to-date with the latest trends and best practices in programmatic SEO to remain competitive in the ever-evolving digital marketing landscape.

Epilogue:

As the world of SEO continues to evolve and become more complex, the need for automation and data science has become more important than ever. By using the techniques and strategies outlined in Programmatic SEO, you can stay ahead of the curve and achieve better results for your website.

But the journey doesn't end here. As new technologies and trends emerge, it's important to stay up-to-date and continue refining your approach to SEO. By staying curious, adaptable, and open-minded, you can continue to unlock the power of automation and data science to achieve even greater success in the world of search engine optimization.

Thank you for choosing Programmatic SEO as your guide on this journey, and we wish you all the best in your SEO endeavors.

www.ingramcontent.com/pod-product-compliance
Lightning Source LLC
Chambersburg PA
CBHW071143220526
45467CB00015B/1787